Making the Father of the Bride's Speech

John Bowden

To Alicia and Stuart ... for accepting me into the family

Every effort has been made to identify and acknowledge the
sources of the material quoted throughout this book. The author
and publishers apologise for any errors or omissions, and would
be grateful to be notified of any corrections that should appear in
any reprint or new edition.

First published in 2000 by
How To Books Ltd, Spring Hill House,
Spring Hill Road, Begbroke, Oxford OX5 1RX, United Kingdom
Tel: (01865) 375794 Fax: (01865) 379162
info@howtobooks.co.uk
www.howtobooks.co.uk

First edition 2000
Reprinted 2001, 2002
2003, 2004, 2005 (twice),
2006, 2007, 2008 (twice), 2009, 2010 and 2011

British Library Cataloguing in Publication Data.
A catalogue record for this book is available from
the British Library.

ISBN: 978 1 85703 568 1

Cover design by Baseline Arts Ltd, Oxford
Produced for How To Books by Deer Park Productions, Tavistock
Typeset by Pantek Arts Ltd, Maidstone, Kent
Printed and bound in Great Britain by Bell & Bain Ltd, Glasgow

NOTE: The material contained in this book is set out in good faith for
general guidance and no liability can be accepted for loss or expense
incurred as a result of relying in particular circumstances on statements
made in this book. Laws and regulations are complex and liable to
change, and readers should check the current position with the relevant
authorities before making personal arrangements.

Contents

Preface

This essential little handbook is written specifically and exclusively for the father of the bride. It will show you how to prepare a unique, relevant and memorable speech that includes just the right balance of emotion, seriousness and humour. And it will supply you with a rich selection of stories, jokes and quotations you may wish to use or adapt.

This is a day charged with emotional intensity. You need to open your heart and display your feelings. Ask yourself: Do I really want the guests to know every last detail of my daughter's Saturday morning tap-dancing lessons, or do I want to share something profoundly meaningful and joyous in our otherwise crazy world? Well, which would you prefer to hear?

John Bowden

1 ▶ Learning the Essentials

The bride's father should be solid, thoughtful and sensible – but he must also allow the lighter, more humorous side of his personality to shine through.

In this chapter:
- ➤ Confirming the programme
- ➤ Knowing your purpose
- ➤ Getting the tone right
- ➤ Remembering the golden rules

So you will be 'saying a few words' on your daughter's big day. The problem is we don't get much practice, do we? That's why this first chapter gets right back to basics by reminding you, or perhaps telling you for the first time about the **essential requirements** of a successful bride's father's speech.

By all means crack a joke or two, if that's your style, but never hide behind your humour. Do not be afraid or ashamed to share poignant, personal moments with the guests. Emotion is an invisible chain that links person to person, regardless of age, gender, race, background or creed.

The audience is on your side. They are not a jury. They are willing you to do well. And, quite frankly, they won't give a damn if you fluff a line or two. What they *will* mind, though, is if it becomes embarrassingly obvious that you have not even bothered to take the time or effort to find out what is expected of you.

 Is this you?

➤ I've never spoken in public before. Help!
➤ I know I'm supposed to be sensitive and sincere but I'm not sure what message, if any, I'm supposed to convey.
➤ I've been told that all I need to say is how I genuinely feel. Is that all there is to it?
➤ I want to make a speech that has real impact.
➤ What I really need is a simple checklist of do's and don'ts for a bride's father's speech.

➤1 Confirming the programme

Traditionally, the **bride's father** opens the chatting, playing most of his delivery with a straight bat. You need to come across as solid, thoughtful and sensible. But you also need to show that there is a lighter, more humorous side to your personality. Let the guests know how much you care for your daughter and how confident you are that she and your new son-in-law will have a wonderful new life together.

Next comes the **bridegroom** who's expected to be a little more adventurous. He needs to show that he understands the importance and significance of the occasion, yet he needs to be quite amusing too.

> Each of the main wedding speeches should have its own individual character, content and tone.

Finally comes the **best man**. His speech should contain plenty of humorous asides and friendly digs about the bridegroom, but these should all be underpinned with a few congratulatory thoughts and optimistic remarks.

However, this conventional pattern of speeches is becoming somewhat outdated. For example, it assumes that the bride was brought up by two parents – and today over two million people in Britain haven't been. And things have changed socially and culturally too – girl power and all that. Today far more women than ever literally want to speak for themselves.

So now it's perfectly acceptable for speeches to be made by other people instead of, or as well as, the traditional big three – perhaps by a **close family friend**, by the **bride's mother**, by the **bride and groom jointly**, or by the **bride** herself. It all depends on the particular circumstances, attitudes and backgrounds of the newlyweds.

The speeches usually begin after the guests have finished eating. Their glasses should be charged *before* anyone speaks.

If there is a toastmaster, he will say something like: 'Ladies and Gentlemen, pray silence for Mr Ben Nevis who will propose a toast to Mr Sydney and Mrs Pearl Harbour.' If there is no toastmaster, the best man often performs the role, but usually in a less formal manner: 'Ladies and Gentlemen, please be silent as Mr Ben Nevis proposes a toast to Mr Sydney and Mrs Pearl Harbour.'

> The important thing is to arrange the programme of speeches and let everyone know where they will fit into it.

➤ **2 Knowing your purpose**

The main purpose of every wedding speech is to propose a toast or to respond to one, or to do both.

➤ **The bride's father (or close family friend, relative or god-father)**: proposes a toast to the bride and groom.

➤ **The bridegroom (possibly with the bride)**: responds to the toast and then proposes a second toast.

➤ **The best man (or best girl)**: responds to the second toast on behalf of the bridesmaids (and any other attendants). He or she may also decide to wind up with a toast to the bride and groom.

➤**3** Getting the tone right

This is an important day for your daughter, for you and for the rest of your family. Your speech should reflect this. It should be:

➤ **Emotional:** you should feel free to display strong personal feelings. Describe an incident or two that demonstrates the joy you and your wife have had in bringing up your daughter and the pleasure you have found in getting to know your new son-in-law – and his parents. However, you

> Don't tell them, show them! Relate a couple of stories that illustrate your powerful, heartfelt feelings.

must be genuine. False heartiness, cheap sincerity and – worst of all – crocodile tears will all be obvious to an audience.

➤ **Optimistic:** this is not the time to share your personal woes, paint a gloomy picture of the present or offer dire predictions about the future. Stress your certainty that in her husband's care, your daughter will prosper along with him and – with a little homily on the 'give and take' neces-

> Always look on the bright side of life!

sary to a successful marriage – the confidence you have that happiness must accompany the love they so evidently bear for one another.

➤ **Enlivened with humour:** inject a little humour into your speech. You do not need to be a stand-up comedian, indeed you should not be. But you must allow the humorous side of your personality to shine through. Some of us are naturally witty. But most of us are not. If you cannot tell jokes, then recall amusing personal anecdotes. They always go down well provided they are used in context and the point of the story is obvious.

> People are always relaxed by humour. It creates that all-important ingredient: instant comfort.

➤ **A tribute to the happy couple:** refer to some positive characteristics of both bride and groom which are *well known* to the audience (perhaps speak of your 'devoted daughter' and her 'hard-working husband'). Then declare your confidence that they will make all the effort needed and will not be found wanting. This is a marriage made in heaven. They were made for each other!

> All your complimentary remarks must have the ring of truth about them. The rule is: characteristic leads to tribute, never vice versa.

➤4 Remembering the golden rules

This simple ten-point plan will ensure the contents of your speech will be memorable – and for the right reasons!

➤ Thank everyone for coming to celebrate your daughter's big day.

➤ Say a few affectionate words about the bride and groom.

➤ Stress the joy you and your wife have had in bringing up your daughter.

➤ Relate one or two amusing or serious incidents from her childhood.

> Just about everything we do in life is governed by rules. Making the bride's father's speech is no different.

➤ Talk of the pleasure you have found in getting to know your new son-in-law and his parents.

➤ Offer some (possibly amusing) thoughts about love and what makes a happy marriage.

➤ Declare your confidence that the bride and groom will make all the effort needed and will not be found wanting.

➤ Learn your opening and closing lines by heart but rehearse the rest of your speech not to be perfect, but to be comfortable. If you feel comfortable, so will the audience.

➤ Try to wrap your speech up within five to ten minutes. Leave them wanting more.

➤ Relax and enjoy the moment!

Checklist

    ✓ Arrange the order of speeches and confirm that you will be setting the ball rolling.

    ✓ Don't forget to include that toast!

    ✓ Keep the overall tone sincere, sensible and sober, but lighten your speech occasionally by injecting little touches of humour.

    ✓ Follow the bride's father's ten golden rules and you won't go far wrong.

2 Being Sober and Sensitive

What can make your speech gripping is its potential to involve the audience on a subjective level, to make them empathise with your deepest feelings, to forge a bond between them and you.

In this chapter:

➤ Conveying emotion and seriousness
➤ Choosing the right stories
➤ Weaving in a couple of quotations

As father of the bride, you are *expected* to indulge in a little emotional outpouring as you say how much you care for your daughter, declare your confidence that she has made the right choice of husband and include a few positive thoughts about love and marriage in general. The problem is that an unremitting, relentless stream of gushing, florid language can come across as pretentious and insincere.

The simple, yet highly effective solution to this apparent dilemma is to **use sincerity and emotion with caution and restraint**, to spread them thinly throughout your speech, like caviar, not pile them on thickly, like marmalade. One or two short, sharp, sensitive, deeply emotional expressions of your strong personal feelings will be far more effective and memorable than a whole series of half-hearted passing references to the pleasure and delight you are experiencing on this most happy of days.

Is this you?

➤ I simply want to express my feelings to our guests.
➤ Of course I want to share a few personal thoughts, but I want to do so in a way that doesn't make me sound like a complete wally.
➤ I'm not too sure how serious to get.
➤ I'm told I'm supposed to, but I don't feel comfortable using soppy, excessively sentimental language.
➤ I want my speech to be emotional yet witty.

➤1 Conveying emotion and seriousness

It's all very well *saying* how much you care for your daughter, how confident you are that she has made the perfect choice of husband and how sure you are that they will have a wonderful future life together. The audience may well think 'How nice', but they won't be moved.

There is an old story about a man who complained to his wife that the trouble with women is that they always take things personally. 'Well I don't!' she replied, unwittingly falling into the trap he had set for her. Brides' fathers are just as likely to dwell on their own feelings and reactions and can be stunned to discover that no one else in the room can relate to their genuine sentiments. 'But I was almost in tears as I was saying this,' they protest. 'How could the guests not be similarly moved?'

How indeed? The problem is that our **feelings are abstract**. It is not that we do not hear or understand abstractions, but without a visual peg, without something we can conjure up in our minds with colour and form, intangible ideas and concepts make little impact and are soon forgotten. Go around an art gallery and note the length of time a lively, realistic portrait will hold your attention in comparison with a piece of modern art which may hardly merit a second glance.

> We hear abstract words like love and devotion with our ears but our brain can no more hang onto them than it could to a soap bubble.

To illustrate this, take a look at the following two lists:

List One	List Two
Joy	Ship
Tenderness	Tree
Delight	Uncle
Happiness	Ice cream
Beauty	Table

Now, put the book down for a moment and see how many of these words you can jot down from memory. You probably remembered more words from List Two. This is because all the words in that list are all *tangible objects*, whereas the ones in List One are *abstract*.

Two further factors are involved here, and neither has anything to do with the audience's hardheartedness. Firstly, when we try to describe the physical symptoms associated with a particular emotion – be it sadness, happiness, or delight – there is little room for surprise. We all know how it feels first hand.

The paradox is that in order to hold an audience's attention we need to provide some new or profound angle, spin or insight into these emotions. Yet how can we say something different and meaningful about what are universal feelings?

Secondly, no matter how original your description of your emotions, it does not alter the fact that those emotions belong to *you*, not to *them*.

So what is the solution? It is to be reticent about your feelings and focus instead upon an incident which illustrates them. Concentrate, not on the emotion that was evoked, but on the situation that gave rise to it. **Turn abstract ideas into strong, concrete visual images**.

> What you must do is take the listener by the hand and guide him or her through your valley of emotions without ever having to mention any of those emotions by name.

Don't bore your listeners with long introductions or unnecessary explanation. Get straight to the heart of the matter. Focus on a single incident or situation; provide a snapshot and it will keep the image alive in your audience's mind and heart.

'I keep all my important certificates and awards in a drawer in the living room – my 1981 BSc, my 1986 accountancy qualification, my 2010 Salesman of the Year award. But shall I tell you which certificate I treasure most? Compared to this one all the others pale into insignificance. I won it back in 1992, well actually I won it jointly. You can keep the BSc, the ACA and the Salesman of the Year ... my most treasured award is the one for first place in the 1992 (*daughter's school*) Father and Daughter Egg and Spoon Race. That award means more to me than a Nobel Prize or an Oscar. We were a real team that day. And, (*daughter*), I want you to know that you'll *always* be in first place in my heart.'

> People want more than to listen to stories, however well they may be told. They also want to experience one or two good, soul-satisfying lingering emotions.

Think of your favourite books, music, films. Don't they all share this lingering quality? Too many speakers try to tell too much, and too much of what they tell is not unique. If they drone on

> Describe a single, uncomplicated, poignant scene which your audience can visualise.

interminably about ballet lessons, pony riding or the Brownies, is it really surprising when listeners lose interest and mentally switch off?

'I must admit it, I didn't want the car to stop today. I wanted to tell the chauffeur to drive on past the church. I know I was selfish, but I didn't want the car to stop. But deep down I knew it had to. I knew it was the right time to walk down the aisle and hand over (daughter) to (son-in-law's) loving and devoted care. And, as I've got to know (son-in-law) well over the last few months, I've come to the inescapable conclusion that this will be very, very good care. Yes, on reflection, I was selfish: it was the right time for the car to stop and for me to get out and walk away.'

> The right mental image can pack a real emotional punch. Your aim is to use words and images that linger in the mind and refuse to disappear.

➤2 Choosing the right stories

As the writer C.S. Forrester reminds us, 'There is no denying the fact that words spoken from the full heart carry more weight than all the artifices of rhetoric.'

You may already have a pretty good idea what incidents you are going to describe. If so, fine. If not, choose ones that have a telling point, ones that will have a positive effect on your audience and will stick in their memories.

The best way to recall some poignant and illuminating episodes is to think about one or two of these memory joggers:

Memory joggers

➤ Birthdays

➤ Turning points

➤ Major decisions

➤ School

➤ College

➤ First job

➤ Illness

➤ Influential people

➤ Holidays

➤ Christmas

➤ Friends

➤ Hobbies

➤ Ambitions

➤ Games and toys

➤ Pets

➤ Travel

Pour yourself a drink, take a hot bath or go for a long walk and the memories will come flooding back. Better still, sleep on it. You really will get some of your best ideas this way. Your subconscious mind will take over and will come up with a whole series of interesting and unexpected memories and connections.

Choose uncomplicated stories that illustrate your daughter's greatest personal qualities, and that consequently will have the greatest emotional impact on your audience.

➤3 Weaving in a couple of quotations

Everyone enjoys hearing a particularly witty or wise turn of phrase or an apt quotation. The **right words** can illuminate your thoughts in a most telling way and really lift your speech. But they must be the right words.

Try to avoid anything remotely negative, sneering or cynical. The problem is, many of the best quotes about love and marriage *are* negative, sneering or cynical. If you feel you really must use one or two, because they are so funny or so appropriate, reverse them to show the sentiment expressed most definitely does *not* apply to the happy couple.

> 'Some cynic once said happiness in marriage is just a lottery. He was wrong. I know *(daughter and son-in-law)* well, I can tell you without a shadow of doubt, they have both hit the jackpot!'

Quotations are intended to promote smiles and nods rather than a strong emotional reaction or helpless mirth. They may well describe some profound and universal truth, but they are not uniquely relevant to your circumstances and the background to this wedding. Not only that, by definition, they are someone else's words, not your own. For these reasons, one or two quotes are plenty enough for any wedding speech.

Very few quotes will be received with a knee-slapping bellylaugh or will cause a lump in the throat. Their merit usually lies in their encapsulation of a truth, a smart observation or a humorous example.

Quoting people can also sound pompous. Just give a couple of appropriate lines and do it in a very casual way. If you are quoting someone famous, it is a good idea either to make it clear you had to look it up or give the impression you're not absolutely sure of your source:

> 'I am reminded of the words of William Shakespeare – reminded I should say by Barbara, who looked it up last night …'

> 'Wasn't it Lord Byron who wrote that …?'

> 'I think it was Thomas Hardy who observed that …'

If you want to quote someone less well known, don't mention him or her by name. If you do, the reaction will probably be an audible 'Who?' Rather, say something like: 'Someone once said …' or 'It has been said that …'

Alternatively, you could attribute the quotation to someone more famous. Oddly enough, this ploy will immediately increase your audience's appreciation of those words of wit and wisdom. But make sure the person you name sounds as if he or she *could* have said that. As Bob Monkhouse didn't say, 'The key is to cause an emotional reaction in your audience, not necessarily to be factually accurate.'

> In speechmaking, we work back from Newton's Law that every action has an equal and opposite reaction. We decide the reaction we want and then work back to choose the words that will produce it.

Here are just a few quotes on love and marriage, which may or may not be right for your speech. If they're not quite in tune with what you're trying to say or how you're trying to say it, fast forward to Chapter 7, where you're certain to find one or two quotes that would work well in your speech.

To the happy couple

'Today is the first day of the rest of your life' (Anon).

'Let those love now who never loved before,
And those who always loved now love the more'
(Robert Burton).

'Here's to matrimony, the high sea for which no compass has yet been invented' (Heinrich Heine).

Marriage

'A happy marriage has in it all the pleasures of a friendship, all the enjoyments of sense and reason, and, indeed, all the sweets of life' (Joseph Addison).

'Two things doth prolong thy life: A quiet heart and a loving wife' (Anon).

'The most important things to do in this world are to get something to eat, something to drink and somebody to love you' (Brendan Behan).

Wisdom

'The essence of love is creative companionship, the fulfilment of one life by another' (John Erskine).

'There is no remedy for love but to love more' (Henry D. Thoreau).

'Let there be spaces in your togetherness ...
Love one another, but make not a bond of love:
Let it rather be a moving sea between the shores of your souls.
Fill each other's cup but drink not from one cup' (Kahlil Gibran).

Checklist

✓ The most powerful bridge between a speaker and his audience is emotion. When a listener feels the emotion of your words, that listener is hooked.

✓ The trick is not to talk about your feelings, but to describe an incident or two that gave rise to them.

✓ Include one or two romantic, sentimental or humorous quotations which seem particularly apt given the couple's personal circumstances and background.

3 Saying It With Humour

A little humour can help lighten that air of intensity so often associated with the bride's father's speech.

In this chapter:

➤ Making humour work for you
➤ Seeing the funny side of things
➤ Offering some words of advice

People can only take so much emotion. They soon begin to display all the classic symptoms of sentiment fatigue: yawning, fidgeting, talking. Sure, they want – and expect – to experience some good, old fashioned soul-satisfying emotion, but they also want to sit back, have a good time and be entertained. So keep them happy by enlivening your sentimental passages with **touches of humour**.

Choose your material with ingenuity and reconsider it with care. Does the humorous line arise naturally from the serious words that precede it? Does its punchline act as a punctuation at the end of a paragraph so that you can embark smoothly on the next topic?

Always try to use jokes and stories that have a telling point. In that way, if you fail to win a laugh, you can go right on talking as if you never meant to. Then it appears that the only reason for saying what you did was its message. If they don't laugh, they won't know they haven't!

 Is this you?

➤ I want my speech to include a few funny bits, but I'm not a naturally funny person.
➤ My family and the groom's family hardly know each other. How can I create a speech which they will all find amusing and entertaining?
➤ I don't want my speech to be too intense. I want it to be amusing as well.
➤ Is it OK to make a few jokes about my daughter?
➤ I need to find one or two humorous and relevant pieces of advice to proffer.

➤1 Making humour work for you

The central dilemma facing many speakers may be put thus: I want to be funny, but I'm not a comedian. Unless you are a gifted comic, you can take the much simpler but equally effective course to win your laughs – play it straight. Leave broad comedy performance to the professional clowns. For most of us, the best way to tell a joke or relate an anecdote is to do so seriously and to follow these tricks of the trade:

➤ **Don't apologise for your inexperience:** avoid lines like 'I don't tell jokes too well, but I'll do my best'. This destroys your humour even before you start.

➤ **Keep it short and simple (KISS):** at a wedding, half the crowd may not know the other half. If you include unnecessary detail or drag the story out at least half your audience will lose interest.

➤ **Allow your guests enough time to enjoy the joke:** if you rush the delivery, you're undercutting the effect you worked so hard to achieve.

➤ **Speak slowly and clearly:** make sure the audience can understand every word of your joke – especially the punchline.

➤ **Enjoy yourself:** smile and look happy. Your mood will be contagious, making it that much easier for you to get a laugh.

> Have you any funny faces, impersonations or mannerisms of speech which infallibly convulse friends and relatives at parties? These eccentricities, suitably broadened out, might work just as well at the reception.

But we all have *some* abilities and talents. Don't hide your light under a bushel. Any regional accents or dialects which you can do well (and only if you *can* do them well) should be incorporated into your stories. A punchline is doubled in effect in the appropriate Cockney or Brummie accent, especially after a 'straight' and serious build up.

➤2 Seeing the funny side of things

Here are some lines that you could use or adapt to take a few friendly little pot shots against yourself, your daughter, son-in-law and wife. You'll find plenty more gags in Chapter 7.

Yourself

Any speaker who cannot laugh at himself leaves the job to others. Poke fun at yourself before you poke fun at anyone else:

'What a panic yesterday evening! I heard (*daughter*) say to her mother, "Mum, I've still got so much to do and I want everything to be perfect. I'm determined not to overlook even the most insignificant detail." And her mother replied, "Don't worry, love, I'll make sure your father's there." '

'As we were on our way to the wedding this morning, (*wife*) turned to me and said, "You know, you don't seem quite as well dressed as when we were married 30 years ago." I replied, "Well I don't know why not, I'm wearing the same suit." '

'I shall never forget my marriage because I had to ask my wife's father permission to marry his daughter. "Have you the means to make her happy?" he asked, "Well," I said, "it'll make her laugh and I'm afraid that's the best I can do." '

'I asked my wife if she remembered our wedding night. ("*Your name*"), she said, "that was 30 years ago, there's no need to apologise now." '

'One evening, after we'd been married for about a month, I asked, "You don't mind if I point out a few of your faults, do you?" "Not at all," she replied, "it's those little faults that stopped me from getting a better husband." '

'When (*daughter*) was in one of her disobedient moods her mother told her to behave herself. "I will for a fiver", replied (*daughter*). (*Wife*) said, "You should be good for nothing — just like your father." '

'I'd like to thank Moss Bros for the suit; Marks and Sparks for the bow tie and Boots for the Valium ...'

Your daughter

Don't forget that it's her big day. And a few crass words can shatter it. Target your humour with extreme caution and care:

'Today I gave away my daughter ... and you will never believe the pleasure that gave me ... or the panic that I felt when I realised how these words could be misinterpreted.'

'I haven't lost a daughter ... I've gained an overdraft.'

'I haven't lost a daughter ... I've gained a bathroom.'

'(*Daughter*) admits that she does have some faults, but she insists that ever being wrong isn't one of them.'

'(*Daughter*) never loses her temper, but occasionally she mislays it.'

Your son-in-law

Once again, don't be too cruel and be aware of how he – and his family – are likely to react to any ribbing:

'(*Son-in-law*) asked if I thought he was old enough to marry (*daughter*). "Oh yes," I replied, "because you'll age fast enough." '

'I warned my new son-in-law that when asked the question, "How's the wife?" the answer expected is *not* "Compared with what?" '

'In many ways (*son-in-law*) has been like a son to me ... he doesn't take any notice of what I say and is threatening to eat us out of house and home.'

'Life could be a bit quiet from now on for (*son-in-law*) because I understand that (*his parents*) gave him strict instructions as a young lad never to go out with married women.'

'And, (*son-in-law*), as you look to the future, remember those wise words from *Monty Python's Flying Circus*: "And now for something completely different ..." '

Your wife

Use one or more of the following lines if – and only if – it is likely to be received by your good lady in the humorous spirit that you no doubt intended!

'I'll never forget my wedding day. You never saw two happier people ... than her mother and father.'

'When we got married (*wife*) didn't have a rag on her back. But she's got plenty of them now.'

'Being a romantic sort of girl, (*wife*) insisted on getting married in her grandmother's dress. She looked absolutely fabulous – but her poor old granny nearly froze to death.'

'Thirty-five years ago I asked for (*wife's*) hand . . . and its been in my pocket ever since.'

'For 25 years my wife and I were deliriously happy ... then we met.'

'I knew my wife could keep a secret because we had been engaged for three months before I even knew anything about it.'

'I told my wife that we hadn't been able to agree on anything during our 27 years of marriage. "28 years," she replied.'

'The first part of our marriage was blissfully happy. Then, on the way home from the ceremony ...'

'I told my wife that I didn't believe in combining marriage with a career – which is why I haven't worked since my wedding day.'

'A few weeks after we got married I came home from work to find (wife) in tears. "I feel terrible," she said. "When I was pressing your suit, I burned a hole in the seat of your trousers." "Don't worry about it," I said. "You've forgotten that I have an extra pair of trousers for that suit." "Oh, I remembered all right," she replied, "I cut a piece from them to patch the hole." '

'Some people ask the secret of our long marriage. We take time to go out to a restaurant twice a week. A little candlelight, dinner, soft music and dancing. She goes Tuesdays, I go Fridays.'

➤**3** Offering some words of advice

Finally, here are some not-too-serious pearls – or rather trinkets – of wisdom which you may wish to impart:

To the bridegroom

'Try praising your wife, even if it does frighten her at first.'

'Advice to the bridegroom? Easy. When she hands you a dishcloth, blow your nose and hand it back.'

To the bride

'Whenever you introduce your husband to someone, refer to him as your first husband – that should keep him on his toes.'

'Remember that although you are now married, your husband would still enjoy a visit to (*local football team*) and an occasional night out with the lads. Let him know you appreciate this. Mention what he's missing every now and then.'

To the happy couple

'Remember that marriage teaches you loyalty, forbearance, self-restraint and many other qualities you wouldn't need if you stayed single.'

'Always remember that money comes first and last. You've got to make it first and then make it last.'

'Never go to bed mad. Stay up and fight.'

'And a word of advice to you both: The best way to get the last word in any argument is to say "sorry".'

'Laugh and the world laughs with you, snore and you sleep alone.'

Checklist

✓ Humour helps relax you and your guests. It also lightens the mood and makes your serious points the more poignant.

✓ Tell a few gentle jokes about yourself – and possibly your daughter, son-in-law and wife. But be careful not to cross that sensitive line. If in doubt, leave it out.

✓ Intermix a few jokey pieces of advice with your more serious offerings.

4 ▶ Beginning and Ending in Style

There is no such thing as the best opening lines or the best closing lines for a bride's father's speech, because every speech – and every speaker – is different.

In this chapter:

➤ Grabbing their attention
➤ Ending on the right note
➤ Proposing a toast to the happy couple
➤ Bracketing your speech

Think of your speech as a gourmet meal. Your opening lines should serve up a tasty little starter that really whets the audience's appetite for the main course. Your closing words should provide a delectable and memorable dessert with a delicious aftertaste.

In this chapter you will learn a number of techniques that can be used to open and close your speech. They are all tried and tested, so you don't need to worry about choosing a dud.

Study the options and decide what would work best for *your* speech – and for *you*.

Work on your chosen lines until they suit your style and have exactly the effect you are after. Then **memorise** them or write them out on a card to use as a prompt. You must know *precisely* how you are going to open and close your speech. There is absolutely no room for any ad-libbing here.

> **? Is this you?**
>
> ➤ The only opening and closing lines I can come up with are 'Good afternoon, Ladies and Gentlemen', and 'Thank you.'
> ➤ I need to find an opening line that will make the audience laugh and make me relax.
> ➤ I want to end my speech with an emotionally-charged big finish.
> ➤ When I rehearse my speech I find myself repeatedly announcing the end, which never seems to come!
> ➤ I want to top-and-tail my speech to make it sound really professional.

➤1 Grabbing their attention

Successful speechmakers often ponder, consciously and unconsciously, for days over their opening words. They know that the first three sentences of their speech set the course for success or failure: a good start points towards plain sailing, a bad one makes you sail against the wind.

For the father of the bride, undoubtedly the most useful varieties of hook are:

➤ the anniversary hook

➤ the quotation hook

➤ the humour hook.

> It is vital to have an opening line that really grabs your audience's attention. Entertainers call this having a hook.

The anniversary hook

There's nothing like telling people what a special day it is today. You're telling them that 'Today's the Day!' As always, use your own words, but this is the sort of thing you should say:

'Ladies and Gentlemen, this is a truly historic day! This day, the 12th of December, will always be remembered because of three world-famous events. Ol' Blue Eyes, the late and great Frank Sinatra was born back in 1915, Muhammad Ali was voted the greatest sportsman of the twentieth century in 1999, and on this day in 201X, (groom) married (bride)!'

'Ladies and Gentlemen, this is a day heavy with significance! This day, the 18th of June, will always be associated with three earth-shattering events. Napolean finally met his Waterloo at Waterloo in 1815, Sir Paul

McCartney had his first day on earth in 1942, and on this day in 201X, you heard the finest wedding speech of your entire lifetime! Now ... who's going to make it?'

You can find plenty of birthdays and anniversaries listed in specialist anniversary books. You'll also find them in most daily and Sunday newspapers.

The quotation hook

The right quotation, told at the beginning of your speech, can illuminate your thoughts in a most telling way and set the tone for what is to follow:

'Ladies and Gentlemen, "Love is the great force in life, it is indeed the greatest of all things." So said E.M. Forster, and E.M. knew what he was talking about ...'

'Ladies and Gentlemen ... Friends, "We cannot fully enjoy life unless someone we love enjoys it with us." Not my words, I'm afraid, although how I agree with them ...'

Sometimes a quotation associated with the bride's or bridegroom's occupation can be adapted to make an excellent and original opening. For example, here are a couple of adaptations suitable for members of the armed services:

'Ladies and Gentlemen, "When she was a lass she served her term. As an office girl to an Attorney's firm. She cleaned the windows and she swept the floor. And she

polished up the handle of the big front door. She polished
up that handle so carefullee. That now she's the ruler of
the Queen's navee". ... Well, almost, anyway ...'

'Ladies and Gentlemen, "Some talk of Alexander, and some
of Hercules, of Hector and Lysander and such great names
as these." But I would rather talk about Captain and Mrs
Mainwaring ... about David and Victoria ...'

The humour hook

If you open with a joke your audience will expect much more
of the same to follow. So use this hook only if you are a naturally humorous person and if you intend your speech to
continue largely in the same light-hearted vein.

Here then are a few jokey openings suitable for the more
modern-minded father of the bride.

'Ladies and Gentlemen, (groom) just asked me, "Would
you like to speak now, or should we let our guests enjoy
themselves a little longer?" '

'Ladies and Gentlemen, unaccustomed to public speaking
as I am, I feel this irresistible urge to prove it.'

'Ladies and Gentlemen, the last time I spoke at a
wedding someone at the rear shouted, "I can't hear you!"
– and a man sitting next to me yelled back, "I'll change
places with you!" '

'Ladies and Gentlemen, the last time I made a wedding speech a man fell asleep. So I asked a page boy to wake him and do you know what the cheeky young so-and-so replied? He said, "You wake him. You were the one who put him to sleep." '

So those are the three types of hook which are most likely to meet your needs. But consider other ideas too. Look for a method that **fits your personality**. Then **test your opening**. Have you used just the right words, in the right order, with the right timing? If you can leave it out altogether and it's not a loss, look for a better one. Now **memorise** and **practise** it.

> Your opening sentence is the second most important sentence of your speech. Yes, you've guessed it: the most important sentence is your last.

➤2 Ending on the right note

The conclusion of a speech is an even bigger opportunity than your opening. People remember longest the last thing they hear. A bad ending can ruin even the best speech; a good ending can salvage even a mediocre one.

Try to end with a flourish. Your concluding remark should be to a speaker what a high note is to a singer: the candescence that triggers spontaneous cheers and applause.

There are many ways to wind up a speech. However, remember that **every speech needs its own ending**, tailored to its content, participants and atmosphere. The following list therefore is intended as no more than a broad spectrum of possibilities:

> The ending, like the opening, is too important to be left to the mercy of chance or the whim of the moment.

➤ the sentimental close

➤ the inspirational close

➤ the wit and wisdom close.

The sentimental close

Your speech will be greatly enhanced by a dramatic, passionate ending. But drama and passion are only partly in the performance. Eloquence demands the appropriate language, a sense of poetry:

'Love is like quicksilver in the hand. Leave the fingers open and it stays; clutch it, and it darts away.'

'Youth's for an hour,
Beauty's a flower.
But love is the jewel that wins the world.'

'Your love makes Vesuvius look like a damp sparkler.'

The inspirational close

We can learn much from the great inspirational speakers of past and present. If you can find an ideal uplifting line that would wrap up your speech perfectly, then grab it, adapt it and use it:

'We wish you happiness that grows, love that deepens and peace that endures. May you cherish each other forever.'

'As you join your lives as one, we hope the special days have just begun. We wish you a lifetime of happiness with one another.'

'Marriage is a constant journey of understanding, fun, sorrow, forgiveness, laughter, sharing. In short, it is a journey of life; a journey of love. May your journey be a long one filled with joy.'

The wit and wisdom close

Some speakers end with a humorous line while others prefer to impart a pearl of wisdom. Why not do both? Why not use laughter to illustrate a universal truth?

> A shrewdly chosen line or verse which combines truth with fun is a far more popular finale than a glum old proverb.

These three 'let-me-leave-you-with-this-thought' gems come from Bob Monkhouse, Groucho Marx and Pam Ayres:

'Marriage is an investment that pays dividends if you pay interest.'

'Woman lies to man. Man lies to women. But the best part is when they lie together.'

'Love is like a curry and I'll explain to you,
That love comes in three temperatures: medium, hot and vindaloo.'

If you can find a great little line that would perfectly round off your speech – whether it was first uttered by Trevor McDonald, Donald Trump or Donald Duck – make any little adjustments here and there and speak it aloud with courage, confidence and conviction.

►3 Proposing a toast to the happy couple

Remember that the purpose of your speech is to propose a toast to the bride and groom. All you need to do is to add a few words after your big finish, for example:

'It is customary for the bride's father to offer the newlyweds some profound piece of advice – advice that has been passed down from generation to generation and no doubt been ignored by all of them. So instead I'll simply say to you both: Have a good life. I mean that. Ladies and Gentlemen, please stand, raise your glasses, and drink with me a toast to the health and happiness of (bride and groom). To (bride and groom)!'

'May the wind be always at your back,
The sun overhead in a clear sky
And the one you love by your side.'

'Be to your virtues a little kind,
Be to your faults a little blind.'

'A toast to love and laughter, and happiness ever after.'

'May their joys be as bright as the morning, and their
sorrows but shadows that fade in the sunlight of love.'

'May their joys be as deep as the ocean
And their misfortunes as light as the foam.'

'May the most you wish for
Be the least you get.'

'Here's to the bride and the bridegroom,
We'll ask their success in our prayers,
And through life's dark shadows and sunshine
That good luck may always be theirs.'

'May you have the hindsight to know where you have been,
The foresight to know where you are going,
And the insight to know when you have gone too far.'

'May your hearts be open with patience and love.
May your lives be filled with blessings from above.
May you always share the best that life can provide.
As you spend your lifetime together side by side.'

'May the love you share forever remain as beautiful as the bride looks today.'

'May you grow old on one pillow.'

'Here's to the groom with bride so fair,
And here's to bride with groom so rare.'

'May your love be as endless as your wedding rings.'

'Let us toast the health of the bride;
Let us toast the health of the groom,
Let us toast the health of the bride's father;
The sucker who paid for this room!'

'A toast to my daughter:
Love, be true to her;
Life, be dear to her;
Health, stay close to her;
Joy, draw near to her;
Fortune, find what you can do for her,
Search your treasure-house through and through for her,
Follow her footsteps wherever she may go –
And keep her husband always her beau.'

> Whichever variety of close you choose, don't forget to add that toast!

➤4 Bracketing your speech

This is a device usually associated with seasoned pros. It is designed not only to grab an audience's attention at the *start* of a speech, but also – and at the same time – to set up a situation that can be exploited at the *end*.

The two brackets consists of a **set-up** at the opening of the speech and a **pay-off** at the end. The words you will end with include those planted clearly at the start. Many lyricists use the same trick, establishing a phrase

> The idea of bracketing is to present your speech as a satisfying whole, not just as a series of thoughts, humorous asides and reminiscences.

at the start and repeating a variation of it to round off the last line. This is how master songsmith Sammy Cahn achieved a nice little twist in the tail of *Call Me Irresponsible*:

Set-up: 'Call me irresponsible, call me unreliable, throw in undependable too.'

Pay-off: 'Call me irresponsible, yes I'm unreliable, but it's undeniably true: I'm irresponsibly mad for you.'

Brackets can serve you well in a speech. The words you will end with are planted clearly at the start, like this:

Set-up: 'On a day such as this I hope I can be forgiven for indulging in a little daydreaming – both reminiscing about the past and predicting the future. Today we celebrate a marriage, the union of my daughter (*name*) and her new husband (*name*) ...'

Pay-off: 'Now all this daydreaming must stop; it is time to move on. At the end of my reminiscing, I've come to these inescapable conclusions: (*wife*) and I have done a lot for (*daughter*) ... but she has done even more for us. There is absolutely no doubt in our minds that the time is now right to entrust her to (*groom's*) loving care. And, knowing (*groom*) as we do, we are certain that that will be very, very good care ...'

Notice how the repetition of the words 'daydreaming' and 'reminiscing' together with the repetition of your daughter's and son-in-law's names helps the open-and-closed nature of the brackets and provides a pleasing and memorable symmetry.

> Bracketing a speech is a wonderful way of linking an attention-grabbing opening with an emotionally-charged big finish.

Checklist

Your opening is an opportunity. Grasp it. Devise a strong opening that's spot on for *this speech, this audience* and **you**. If the shoe doesn't fit, don't wear it. There are plenty of shoes that *do* fit.

You must end on a high note: thought-provoking, romantic, inspiring. Plan it well and practise it. The last sentence must come out perfectly. Its the last impression you will leave with your audience.

Don't forget to include that toast!

A speech can be made truly memorable by planting a bracket at the beginning and a matching one at the end.

Putting It All Together

To create a memorable wedding speech requires excitement, empathy, warmth, enthusiasm ... and flair. Flair is the sizzle in the sausage.

In this chapter:

➤ Preparing your script
➤ Using words to be said, not read
➤ Adding a sparkle to your speech
➤ Remembering rhythm
➤ Keeping it flowing

Having something worthwhile to say is *never* enough. You need to know how to use words and images to reach your audience's minds and hearts. Your speech needs **a touch of flair**. Flair is partly intuition – which comes from experience, imagination and a willingness to think – and a careful study of this chapter!

Every communication is an opportunity to throw a bridge across a void. If you can do this, your speech will have more effect than you could ever have believed possible. When we face an important interview, we prepare ourselves to make the best possible impression. We look good. So, when we are about to meet an audience, we should polish our words as well as our shoes. We should sound good.

Today people's expectations are high and their attention spans are low. Merely to gain and hold an audience's attention requires flair. If you want to keep them interested, your speech must sparkle. So let's get polishing.

 Is this you?

➤ I don't know what sort of script to prepare – if any.
➤ The last time I made a wedding speech I think I must have sounded as if I was reading the news. I was too matter of fact.
➤ I want my speech to be more than just an unconnected series of jokes and reminiscences.
➤ Of course I want what I say to convey my emotions and be entertaining, but I also want what I say to sound good.
➤ I want to make a speech I can be truly proud of!

➤1 Preparing your script

The best talkers are those who are the most natural. They are easy, fluent, friendly and amusing. No script for them. How could there be? They are talking only to us and basing what they say on our reactions as they go along. For most of us, however, that sort of performance is an aspiration rather than a description. Our tongues are not so honeyed and our words are less winged. We need a script.

But what sort of script? Cards? Notes? Speech written out in full? It's up to you. There is no right way of doing it. Here is a simple method favoured by many speakers:

➤ Write the speech out **in full**.

➤ **Memorise** the opening and closing lines and **familiarise** yourself with the remainder of the speech.

➤ **Summarise** the speech on one card, or one sheet of paper using **key words** to remind you of your **sequence** of anecdotes, quotations, jokes and so on.

> The main advantage of this method is that the speaker will not only be sure to cover everything he wants to, but also will come across as a natural and spontaneous speaker who is not merely reciting a prepared speech.

➤**2** Using words to be said, not read

Most people can write something to be *read*, few can write something to be *said*. Indeed, most people are unaware that there is even a difference.

We are used to writing things to be read: by our friends, our relatives, our bosses, our work colleagues. Such everyday written communication is known as **text**. What we are not used to doing is speaking our written words aloud. Writing intended to be spoken and heard is known as **script**.

Every effective speaker *must* recognise that there are very important differences between text and script, namely:

Text	Script
➤ is a journey at the reader's pace	➤ is a journey at the speaker's pace
➤ can be re-read	➤ is heard once, and only once
➤ can be read in any order	➤ is heard in the order it is spoken

Therefore, you must prepare a speech for an audience which *cannot* listen at its own pace; which *cannot* ask you to repeat parts it did not hear or understand; and which *cannot* choose the order in which to consider your words.

Consider how the same sentiment might be conveyed by a writer, first using text and then script:

> We seem subconsciously to understand the best words and phrases and the best order of words and phrases when we speak, but we seem to lose the knack when we write script.

Text:

The meaning of marriage is not to be found in church services, or in romantic novels or films. We have no right to expect a happy ending. The meaning of marriage is to be found in all the effort that is required to make a marriage succeed. You need to get to know your partner, and thereby to get to know yourself.

Script:

'The meaning of marriage isn't to be found in wedding bells ... it isn't the stuff of Mills and Boon romances ... there is no happy ever after. No, the meaning of marriage is in the trying and it's about learning about someone else ... and through that learning about yourself.'

The lesson is clear: **speak your words out loud before you commit them to paper**. You will find that each element, each phrase, each sentence, will be built from what has gone before. Instinctively, you will take your listeners from the **known** to the **unknown**; from the **general** to the **particular**; from the **present** to the **future**.

➤**3** Adding a sparkle to your speech

➤ **Paint word pictures**: merely listening to a wordy description, however enthusiastically delivered, is a yawn. Watching a story unfold before your eyes, on the other hand, is dramatic and memorable. The characters move. The scenes are in colour. The whole thing has life. The best writers of today know they must use specific detail to paint word pictures. This comes from *Writing Down the Bones* by Natalie Goldberg:

> Use words and images creatively and imaginatively and your speech will come to life. Things happen in the minds and hearts of your audience. If you look into their eyes, you can see it happen. It's a great experience.

'I was in Costa's Chocolate Shop in Owatonna, Minnesota. My friend sat opposite me. We'd just finished Greek salads and were writing in our notebooks for half an hour among glasses of water, a half-sipped coke, and a cup of coffee with milk. The booths were orange, and near the front counter were lines of cream candies dipped in chocolate. Across the street was the Owatonna Bank, designed by Louis Sullivan, Frank Lloyd Wright's teacher. Inside the bank was a large cow mural and beautiful stained-glass windows.'

> Give the audience the right specific detail and they can see your word picture.

➤ **Use figurative language:** try to make your speech colourful and original. Similes and metaphors are particularly useful devices. A **simile** is a figure of speech, usually introduced by *like* or *as*, that **compares** one thing to another:

'A face like a mixed grill.'

'As soft as primroses.'

Because a simile's function is comparison, it is not as evocative as a metaphor. A **metaphor** does not so much compare as **transform** one thing to another. It is more subtle and revealing, stimulating imagery beyond the original transformation:

'Marriage. Ever since humans gathered together they – we – have displayed a basic instinct for becoming couples. Your man and your woman. Your Romeo and your Juliet. Your yin and your yang. It's as natural as his and hers bath towels. If the life of humankind were music it would be all duets. It's been a bit of a musical day one way and another. Violins in harmony with cellos. (*Daughter*) in harmony with (*son-in-law*). The past in harmony with the future. And, as the Bard of Avon put it: "If music be the food of love, play on".'

Another useful figure of speech is **hyperbole**, or deliberately overstating your argument. In a wedding speech you can get away with saying things that most people would find embarrassing and even crass in everyday conversation:

'You are the best daughter in the world.'

➤**4** Remembering rhythm

A good speech should attract and hold listeners as a magnet attracts and holds iron filings. Here are a few more techniques that will grab your audience and add an enchanting tuneful quality to your speech:

➤ **The rule of three:** three is a magical number. People love to hear speakers talk to the beat of three. The effect of three words, three phrases or three sentences is powerful and memorable:

'Marriage is the meeting of two minds ... of two hearts ... of two souls.'

'May you be blessed with happiness that grows ... with love that deepens ... and with peace that endures.'

'I wish you fun and excitement for today ... hopes and dreams for tomorrow ... and love and happiness forever.'

➤ **Parallel sentences:** sentences that are parallel add a rhythmic beauty that helps an audience anticipate and follow your thoughts.

Using words colourfully and creatively will bring your speech to life like a shot of whisky in a cup of coffee.

'Marriage is a celebration of love. Marriage is a celebration of life. Marriage is a celebration of joy.'

➤ **Alliteration:** the repetition of sounds and syllables, usually at the beginning of words, can help create just the right mood. Your speech will become special and spellbinding:

'Water your garden with friendship and faith and favour. And then watch it grow. You deserve a garden of love.'

➤5 Keeping it flowing

Have you noticed how entertainers, politicians and TV presenters move **easily** and **unobstrusively** from one topic to another? Like them, you can make your speech flow **smoothly** and **gracefully** from beginning to end by making use of a few of these simple devices:

The way a speaker keeps things flowing takes a little thought, but it's so worthwhile in its effect. How often have you winced at a clumsy transition or a hoary cliché: 'Which reminds me of the story of ...'?

➤ **A bridge** is a word that alerts an audience that you are changing direction or moving to a new thought:

'(Daughter) took a job in London. Meanwhile other developments were taking place ...'

➤ **A trigger** is a repetition of the same word or phrase to link one topic with another:

'That was what (daughter) was like at school. Now I'll tell you what she was like at college ...'

➤ **A rhetorical question** is a question which you ask – and answer:

> 'That's what makes our marriage so happy. So what advice can I offer to the newlyweds? ...'

Some members of the audience may know both the bride and the bridegroom very well, while others may only know one of them. Asking a rhetorical question is an excellent way of telling people something while not insulting the intelligence of those already in the know:

> 'What can I tell you about a girl who won the school prize for geography, represented the county at netball and passed her driving test ... at the sixth attempt?'

➤ **A flashback** is a sudden shift to the past to break what seems to be a predictable narrative:

> 'They first met in ...'
> 'They both worked for ...'
> 'They started going out together when ...' (yawn, yawn!)

It would have been far more interesting to have provided an unexpected flashback link, such as:

> 'Today she's the confident, woman-about-town you see before you. But five years ago she wasn't like that ...'

➤ **A list** is a very simple way of combining apparently unrelated incidents:

> 'I remember three occasions when (*daughter*) got into trouble at school ...'

But don't rely too heavily on lists because a catalogue of events soon becomes extremely tedious to listen to.

➤ **A pause** is a non-verbal way of showing your audience that you have finished one section of your speech and are about to move on to another.

➤ **A physical movement** is another non-verbal signal that you are moving on to something new. If you turn to your daughter, the guests will know that you are going to talk to her, or about her.

➤ **A quotation, joke or story** can also serve as an excellent link. Here a man-on-the-bus gag links a personal compliment about your daughter's good manners with a more general observation that everyone has played their part in making this a day to remember.

> '(*Daughter*) always shows good old-fashioned courtesy to her fellow human beings. A rare attribute today, I'm sure you'll agree. When she was on the bus last week she stood up to give an elderly gentleman her seat. He was so surprised he fainted. When he came round he said 'Thank you' and (*daughter*) fainted. Well I'm delighted to say there has been absolutely no shortage of courtesy here today. Things could not have gone better ...'

Checklist

Rehearse using a variety of types of script – cards, notes, speech written out in full – before deciding which method suits you best.

Think like a listener and write like a talker. Speak your words out loud before you commit them to paper. Use *effective* language, not necessarily correct language.

Use words and images creatively and imaginatively so they reach your audience's minds and touch their hearts.

It is important that what you say *sounds* good. Your speech should have its own rhythm. Give it light and shade. A landscape of valleys and peaks will keep an audience interested and involved. People need valleys before they can see peaks.

Make sure your speech flows *smoothly* and *gracefully* from beginning to end.

6 ▶ Delivering Your Speech

This above all: To thine own self be true.

> **In this chapter:**
> ➤ Finding your style
> ➤ Giving out the right non-verbal messages
> ➤ Making fear your friend

What you say is so much more important than how you say it. A speaker without a powerful or melodious voice can register just as convincingly as a great orator as soon as the audience tunes into the fun and caring behind his words.

True, a little judicious advice on delivery technique can help smooth the edges without stifling individuality. Yet a great deal of so-called expert advice will remove the wonderfully imperfect distinctions about us and create unremarkable clones.

So while this chapter will stress the importance of projecting positive language and having the right attitude to your speech, it will **not** put you in a strait-jacket of artificial presentation techniques.

Essentially, you just need to be yourself – but **yourself made large**. If you offer your homage, your humour and your heart to any audience, they cannot resist.

 Is this you?

➤ The last time I made a speech it felt like I was standing aside from myself, listening to a voice that didn't belong to me. It was very strange.
➤ As I stand up in front of an audience a kind of lead veil comes over me and all I can see is a close-up of myself.
➤ When I speak in public, my voice dries up and it destroys all the natural flow, all the rhythms and any kind of creative spark or anecdote that might come in is destroyed.
➤ I think my body language is very negative.
➤ I am extremely nervous about giving this speech.

➤1 Finding your style

It is exceedingly difficult to discuss style and technique in general terms, since the ability to 'hold an audience', to be sober, sensible and sensitive, yet amusing is such a personal business. However, there are certain 'rules' and guidelines which appear to be universal. Here they are:

➤ **Make your speech 'yours'**: did Elvis, Sinatra and Johnny Rotten all sound the same singing *My Way*? Of course not. The artist makes the crucial difference. So, too, does the speaker.

Whatever individual characteristics you have that are special to you should be nurtured and cultivated and worked on, for it is those personal and unique quirks of appearance, personality and expression that will mark you out as a speaker with something different to offer. And that is never a bad thing.

➤ **Be conversational**: sitting at leisure, with family, friends or colleagues, your conversation will be naturally relaxed and chatty, because that is the language of easy communication. When you make the bride's father's speech, the words and phrases you use should be more considered, imaginative, creative and rhythmical than your everyday language, yet the way you say them, the way you deliver your speech should remain unaffectedly relaxed and chatty.

If you 'put on an act', you will be perceived as phoney, boring, or lacking in personality. As a result, you won't come over well. Certainly you may need to speak a little louder or make other concessions to accommodate the needs of your audience, but, in essence, nothing in your delivery style should change.

Casual conversation is not constructed in a literary way. You do not always finish your sentences. You repeat yourself. You use ungrammatical con-structions – but you are obeying a different set of rules. You are obeying the rules of effective spoken communication which have been learnt, instinctively, down the ages. Don't aban-don these rules when you speak in public.

> The key then is to recognise what you are doing when you 'get it right' and achieve any successful communication, be it formal or informal, business or social, and then stay with it in any given situation, regardless of the stress level.

➤ **Being heard**: you must be *audible*. If you are not, all else is lost. If there is public address equipment available, find out how it works, get plenty of practice and then use it. If there is no sound-enhancing equipment, speak as clearly and as loudly as is necessary to be heard. If the only other person in the room was at the back, you would talk to him or her naturally, at the right level, without shouting or strain, by:

➤ keeping your head up

➤ opening your mouth wider than during normal speech

➤ using clearer consonants

➤ slowing down.

If you remember that you must be heard by that same person, at the back, during your speech, however many other people may be in the room, you will make those same four *natural* adjustments to your delivery.

➤2 Giving out the right non-verbal messages

We *speak* with our vocal cords, but we **communicate with our whole body**. An audience does a lot more than listen to a speech – it *experiences* it. Everything about a speaker's manner and demeanor contributes to the overall impression that the audience takes away.

> Body language is potent. When you address a group of people they are constantly responding consciously and unconsciously to what your body is saying to them.

So what hidden messages do you give out when you speak? If you are unsure, watch yourself in a mirror, or get someone to video you. You will probably find that you need to work on one or more of the following:

➤ stance and posture

➤ movement and gestures

➤ eye contact and facial expression.

However, remember that while each of these may be considered in isolation, a positive change made to any of them will also have a direct and immediate positive effect on the others.

Stance and posture are important. You are making a fundamental statement with your body. An aligned, upright posture conveys a message of confidence and integrity.

Movement and gestures you should be far more than just a talking head. You don't want to be so motionless that you look like a statue on loan from Madame Tussaud's. But, equally, you shouldn't attempt an impersonation of racing pundit John McCririck's arm-waving histrionics.

Try to identify any annoying movements or gestures which you display. Do any of these faults apply to you?

➤ playing with your watch

➤ talking with your hand in front of your mouth

➤ pushing your glasses back up your nose

➤ jingling coins in your pocket

➤ waving your hands about for no reason

➤ rustling your notes

➤ shuffling your feet

➤ swaying

➤ making pointless gestures.

Try to eliminate any such habits because they are a powerful means of distraction. Your audience will become preoccupied with them and will start *watching* you rather than *listening* to you.

Eye contact and facial expression are crucial aspects of effective communication because they gain and then maintain an audience's attention, create rapport, and give you valuable feedback as to how well you are coming over.

> The worst you can do, apart from mumbling inaudibly, is not to look at the guests.

Ideally, you will have **memorised** your opening and closing lines, so *look* at your audience as you deliver them. During the middle of your speech, try to keep your head up from your script, or notes for most of the time.

Entertainers use the so-called **lighthouse technique** to maintain eye contact with their audiences. This means beaming all around the room slowly, tracing an imaginary X or Z shape but continually varying the size and shape of the letter to avoid any eye sweeps becoming routine and predictable. Look at everyone and make this deliberate and noticeable. Stop occasionally to look at individuals for just long enough to give the impression that you are talking to them without picking them out for special attention.

But you must do more than simply look at your audience: you must use your eyes and your facial expression to **convey your feelings**. This isn't as difficult as it may sound. You do it every day. Practise using your eyes and facial expression to convey: happiness, optimism, mirth, joy, confidence, sincerity.

There is nothing more captivating than a smile. It shows warmth and friendliness and says, 'I'm really pleased to be making this speech!' So smile, smile – and smile again.

Once you begin to give out positive silent messages about your feelings and emotions, you will become even more enthusiastic and

> Positive body language not only reflects positive feelings, it creates them.

eager – and this, in turn, will be reflected in your body language. You will have broken into a wonderful virtuous circle.

➤ 3 Making fear your friend

Fear is nothing to be frightened of. People get nervous because they are afraid of failing, of looking foolish, and not living up to expectations. Nervousness is caused by the fear of looking ridiculous to others.

Few speakers claim to be able to speak without any nerves. Some will say that lack of nerves is not only unlikely, it is undesirable. They need the adrenalin to carry them along. So how do you make things easier for yourself? First be assured that excessive worry is avoidable, if you follow this advice:

Rehearse

Friends who tell you not to worry should worry you. Don't you believe them when they say, 'No need to rehearse, it'll be all right on the night' – unless your hidden agenda is to get £250 for a camcorder calamity. If you want to calm your nerves and make a great speech, you simply *must* rehearse.

Why do some actors freeze or fumble on the opening night and then pick up a British Theatre Drama Award six months later? It's a fear of unfamiliarity. As

> The more rehearsal, the more the certainty of success and greater peace of mind.

the days, weeks and months go by, the fear abates and the quality of the performance improves.

Words become more familiar. Awkward juxtapositions are smoothed out. You suddenly think of a way of saying a stuffy sentence in a more straightforward and colloquial style. At the same time you will recognise the parts of your speech that hit the spot, the parts that require a little fine tuning, and the parts that are simply not worth including.

As with the type of script you use, so the rehearsal method you employ must be the one that best suits you. Some speakers like to be isolated and unheard in a distant room, with or without a mirror. Others perform their speeches again and again to a sympathetic spouse or friend, either encouraging suggestions from them or requiring nothing more than a repeated hearing to ease away inhibitions.

Rehearse your beginning and ending until you have got them spot on. Rehearse the body of your speech not to be perfect, but to be **comfortable**. Audiences don't expect you to be perfect, but they *need* you to be comfortable. If you're not comfortable, neither are they. And if they're not comfortable, they cannot be receptive to your words of wit and wisdom, however hard they may try.

Have the right attitude

Tell yourself that you are going to make a great little speech. And *believe* it. The largely untapped power of positive thinking really is enormous. It has been estimated that 85 per cent of performance is directly related to **attitude**. Unfortunately, many speakers think they are going to fail and, with this attitude, this becomes a self-fulfilling prophecy.

> As Henry Ford put it: 'Whether you think you will succeed or whether you think you will fail, you will probably be right.'

Visualise success

Visualisation is the planting of mental images into the subconscious mind. These images must be vivid and real – you must be able to *see*, to *hear*, to *smell*, to *touch*, to *taste* and to truly **live them**.

This is not a crankish idea. Controlled medical experiments have proved it to be true. When a patient

> If you can vividly imagine an event happening, it will greatly strengthen the likelihood of it actually happening.

visualises cancer cells being engulfed by anti-bodies in the bloodstream, it is far more likely to happen than if that patient just lies back and lets nature take it course.

So reinforce your positive attitude with a positive visualisation of your speech. Imagine yourself talking in a relaxed and confident manner. You are looking good. They love your opening hook. But it gets better; your stories, reminiscences and little jokes wow them. They are eating out of your hand. Then comes that emotionally charged big finish. Nobody could have topped that. Listen to their cheers and applause. Now that's what I call a wedding speech! What you used to call fear can now be renamed excitement and anticipation.

 Checklist

✓ The challenge is to project your personality, not suppress it. Knowing that you not only *can*, but also *should* 'be yourself' will stop you worrying about your 'performance', and allow you to concenrate on what eally matters: being sober, sensible and sensitive, yet amusing.

✓ The effectiveness of your speech will depend, to a large extent, on your body language. A relaxed stance, upright posture, purposeful economy of movement, fluid gestures and lively eyes and facial expression will all capture your audience's attention and greatly enhance the impact of your speech.

✓ Remember that the greatest antidotes to nerves are preparation and attitude.

7 ▷ Jokes and Quotes for Your Speech

Your speech should be solid, thoughtful and sensible. However, even your most profound, serious and emotional outpourings should be counterbalanced by a few witty asides. You must also allow the lighter, more humorous side of your personality to shine through. The best sort of humour for a bride's father is often self-deprecating. Show the guests that you don't take yourself too seriously. For example:

> 'Janet pleased me by laughing uproariously when reading the draft of this little speech, only to tell me it was my spelling that so amused her.'

Self-mockery of this kind is a subtle demonstration of your underlying confidence (honestly!). It offends nobody and it reminds the crowd what a likeable, loveable chap you really are.

You can also take a few *gentle* pot shots at people sitting along-side you at the top table, so long as you are confident that none of them will be offended. Some examples of humour targeted at yourself, your daughter, new son-in-law and wife can be found between pages 23 and 27.

This chapter provides a miscellany of one-lines, jokes, quotations and stories which you could use, or adapt and personalise, to suit the precise circumstances of the wedding. They are in no logical order because, as we have seen, humour and seriousness work best when intermixed. People respond best to a gag when it follows on naturally from a serious or emotional point ... and vice-versa.

And now it's time for those jokes and quotes:

> A little boy asks his father, 'Daddy, how much does it cost to get married?' His father replies, 'I don't know, son ... I'll let you know when I finish paying.'

> Success in marriage is more than finding the right person; it is being the right person (Rabbi B.R. Bricker).

> Personally, I think one of the greatest things about marriage is that as both husband and father, I can say anything I want around the house. Of course, no one pays the least bit of attention.

> Everything that is exchanged between a husband and wife in their life together can only be the free gift of love. It can never be demanded by one or the other as a right (Ellen Key).

Jack was reading his newspaper after breakfast. He came across an article about a beautiful singer who was about to marry a football player known primarily for his lack of IQ. He turned to his wife and said, 'I'll never understand why the biggest wallies get the most attractive girls.' His wife replied, 'Why thank you, dear.'

Mary told her friend she was going to the doctor's . 'Why? What's wrong?' asked the friend. 'Because I don't like the look of my husband,' Mary replied. 'Can I come with you?' enquired the friend, 'I can't stand the sight of mine either.'

Love, the strongest and deepest element in all life, the harbinger of hope, of joy, of ecstasy; love, the defier of all laws, of all conventions; love, the freest, the most powerful moulder of human destiny (Emma Goldman).

Liz is the most wonderful, charming, intelligent, thoughtful daughter a father could have. She does everything for me. She even wrote this speech.

After all those years together, a husband decided it was time to put a little magic back into their marriage. He disappeared.

Married couples resemble a pair of scissors, often moving in opposite directions, yet always punishing anyone or anything which comes between them (Sydney Smith).

Marriage is the only adventure open to the cowardly (Voltaire).

Good Ladies, afternoon and Gentlemen ... I *knew* I should have rehearsed this speech.

The love we give away is the only love we keep (Elbert Hubbard).

A toast to sweethearts. May all sweethearts become married couples and may all married couples remain sweethearts.

A man asks his wife, 'Why do you always carry a photograph of me in your handbag when you go to work?' She replies that whenever there is a problem she looks at the photo and the problem seems to disappear. 'That shows what a miraculous and powerful influence I have on you,' he boasts. 'No it doesn't,' she retorts. 'When I see your picture I say to myself: What problem can possibly be any greater than this one?'

A good marriage is one which allows for change and growth in individuals (Pearl Buck).

A nagging old woman tells a grumpy old man, 'If you were my husband, I would poison your cocoa.' To which the old chap replies, 'If you were my wife, I'd drink it.'

I haven't spoken to my wife for eighteen months ... it would be rude to interrupt.

In most good marriages, the woman is the husband's closest friend and adviser (Nancy Reagan).

Richard is taking his dog for a walk through the cemetery when he sees a man kneeling at a grave. The man seems to be praying with profound intensity, and keeps repeating, 'Why did you die? Why did you die?' Richard approaches him, and says, 'I don't want to interfere with your private grief, but this demonstration of hurt and pain is more than I have ever witnessed before. For whom do you mourn so deeply? Your child? A parent? Who, may I ask, rests in that grave?' The mourner looks up and answers, 'My wife's first husband ... Why did you die? Why did you die?'

I remember the day so well when Samantha came home from her ballet lesson and announced, 'Mrs Evans said I would be a fine dancer except for two things.' 'What are they?' I asked. And Sam replied, 'My feet.'

Love does not consist of gazing at each other but in looking outward together in the same direction (Antoine de Saint-Exupéry).

Don't let your marriage go stale. Change the bag on the Hoover of life (Victoria Wood).

Father O'Grady is saying his goodbyes to the parishioners, as he always does, after his Sunday morning service. Mary O'Leary comes up to him in tears. 'What's bothering you, my child?' asks Father O'Grady. 'Oh Father, I've got terrible news,' replies Mary, 'My husband passed away last night.' 'Oh Mary,' says the good Father, 'that's terrible. Tell me, Mary, did he have any last requests?' 'Yes,' Mary replies sheepishly, 'he said: "Mary, please put down that gun." '

A man asks his friend, 'Don't you and your wife ever have any differences of opinion?' And the friend replies, 'Of course we do ... but I never tell her about them.'

Man and wife, a king and queen with one or two subjects, and a few square yards of territory of their own: this, really, is marriage. It is true freedom because it is true fulfilment, for man, woman and children (D.H. Lawrence).

I was so proud of Anna. When she was only five she could spell her name backwards.

When Laura was a little girl, she ran to me, sobbing, 'I lost my puppy!' 'Don't cry,' I said, 'We'll get your puppy back. I'll put an ad in the paper.' 'That won't do any good,' Laura wailed, 'Spot can't read!'

I went to the doctor and asked for some sleeping pills for my wife. The doctor asked me, 'Why?' and I said, 'Because she just woke up.'

I'll never forget what started our first argument. Betty said, 'What's on the TV?' And I replied, 'Dust.'

Always remember that the most effective way to remember your wife's birthday is to forget it once.

Do you want me to tell you something really subversive? Love is everything it's cracked up to be. That's why people are so cynical about it (Erica Jong).

A lady placed an ad in the classifieds. It read: 'Husband wanted.' The next day she received over one hundred replies. They all said the same thing: 'You can have mine.'

A man was invited to an old friend's home for dinner. His friend spent the whole evening addressing his wife in the most endearing of terms, calling her Honey, Darling, My Love , Sweetheart, Pumpkin, and the like. The guest was impressed as the couple had been married over thirty years and while the wife was off in the kitchen he said to his old mate, 'I think it's wonderful that after all these years you've been married you can still call your wife those pet names.' His friend hung his head. 'To tell the truth,' he said, ' I forgot her real name years ago.'

We grow old as soon as we cease to love and trust (Louise Honouring de Choiseul).

A man approaches a beautiful woman in a large supermarket and says, 'I can't find my wife. Can you talk to me for a couple of minutes?' 'Why?' she asks. And the man replies, 'Because every time I talk to a beautiful woman, my wife suddenly appears out of nowhere.'

Janet was always pestering us for a DVD player. I told her we couldn't afford one, but she wouldn't take no for an answer. Then one day she came home clutching a package containing a brand new DVD player. 'Wherever did you get the money to pay for that?' I asked. 'It's alright, dad,' she replied, 'I traded in the TV for it.'

A couple were celebrating their golden wedding anniversary. Their domestic tranquillity had long been the talk of the town, and a local newspaper reporter was enquiring as to the secret of their long and happy marriage. 'Well it dates back to our honeymoon,' explained the husband. 'We went horse riding in North Wales. We hadn't gone too far when my wife's horse bucked. My wife quietly said, 'That's once.' A little further the horse bucked again and once more my wife quietly said, 'That's twice.' We hadn't gone another half mile when the nag did it a third time. Without saying a word my wife dismounted and gave the horse an unmerciful kick in the balls. I started to protest over her treatment of the horse, when she looked at me and quietly said, 'That's once ... '

Jacqui was late for school, so I shouted to her, 'Have you got your socks on yet?' 'Yes, dad,' she replied, 'all except one.'

We can only learn to love by loving (Iris Murdoch).

In my youth, I remember asking my beloved, 'Shall we try a couple of new positions tonight?' And she replied, 'That's a wonderful idea, love ... you stand by the sink, and do the dishes ... and I'll lay on the sofa, and fart.'

A man went to the police station, wishing to speak to the burglar who broke into his house the night before. 'You'll get your chance in court,' said the desk sergeant. 'No, no, no!' exclaimed the man, ' I want to know how he got into the house without waking my wife. I've been trying to do that for years.'

Marriage is an armed alliance against the outside world (G.K.Chesterton).

A married couple are enjoying a meal out when a gorgeous blonde walks over to their table, exchanges a warm greeting with the husband, blows him a kiss, and strolls off. 'Who was that?' demands the wife. 'If you must know, that was my mistress,' replies the husband. 'Your mistress? I want a divorce!' screams the wife. 'Are you sure you want to give up a big house in the country, a Mercedes, furs, jewellery and our holiday home in Monte Carlo?' he asks. They continue dining in silence for a while. Finally, the wife asks, 'Isn't that James over there? Who is he with?' The husband replies, 'Why that's *his* mistress.' And the wife says, 'Well, *ours* is definitely sexier.'

Love doesn't just sit there, like a stone, it has to be made, like bread; re-made all the time, made new (Ursula K. LeGuin).

A funeral service is being held for a woman who has recently passed away. At the end of the service the pallbearers are carrying the coffin out when they accidentally bump into a wall, jarring the casket. They hear a faint noise, open the coffin and find the woman is still alive. She lives for ten more years and then really does die. A second service is held at the church, and at the end of the ceremony the pallbearers are again carrying out the casket. As they are walking towards the exit, the husband cries out, 'Watch the wall!'

These three efforts are the golden threads with which domestic happiness is woven: to repress a harsh answer, to confess a fault, and to stop - right or wrong - in the midst of argument (Elizabeth Hidden Estaugh).

My wife asked me to buy organic vegetables from the supermarket. But I wasn't sure if the ones on display were grown naturally, so I grabbed an elderly assistant and said, 'These vegetables are for my wife. Have they been sprayed with any poisonous chemicals?' And the assistant said, 'No. You'll have to do that yourself.'

The best way to get most husbands to something is to suggest that perhaps they are too old to do it (Anne Bancroft).

An elderly man lays dying on his bed when he smells the the aroma of cooked ham wafting up the stairs. It has been his favourite food for the entire sixty years of his marriage. Somehow he finds the strength to stagger to the top of the stairs and calls down to his beloved, 'Thank you, darling, for preparing my favourite meal for the final time.' And she shouts, 'Get back to bed, you old fart. The ham's for your funeral!'

Love may be blind, but marriage is a real eye-opener.

On a cold February morning, a woman walks into a post office and sees a small, balding, middle aged man sticking stamps on envelope after envelope. He then takes a perfume bottle from his briefcase and starts spraying scent all over them. Her curiosity gets the better of her. She goes up to the man and asks what he's doing. He says, 'I'm sending out a thousand Valentine cards, all signed "Guess Who?"' 'But why?' asks the woman. 'I'm a divorce lawyer,' replies the man.

If your wife laughs at your joke, it means you either have a good joke or a good wife.

Love is a general leveller - it makes a king a slave: and inspires the slave with every joy a prince can taste (Elizabeth Inchbald).

When Dave asked me for Jill's hand in marriage, I said, 'Dave, you should know Jill's been asked to get married hundreds of times.' 'Who by?' Dave asked. I replied, 'By me!'

MI5 want to recruit a spy. After extensive interviews and tests, the short-list is down to three. Now they need to test them to the limit. The first candidate is brought to the office of the Head of MI5, on the twentieth floor of the building, and the conversation goes like this: 'Do you love your wife?' 'Yes I do, sir.' 'Do you love your country?' 'Yes I do, sir.' 'Which do you love more, your wife or your country?' 'My country, sir.' 'Then prove it. Your wife is in the next room. Take this gun and kill her!' The man thinks deeply for a few moments and then exclaims, 'No, I can't do that!' and runs out of the office in tears. The second candidate is ushered in. The Head of MI5 asks the same questions and he receives the same replies. 'Then prove it,' says the Head, 'Take this gun and kill your wife!' The man picks up the gun goes into the next room and there is silence for five minutes. He comes back covered in sweat, shaking uncontrollably. He puts the gun down and says, 'I just couldn't do it.' The third candidate comes in and the Head asks the same questions and receives the same replies. 'Then prove it,' says the Head, 'Take this gun and kill your wife!' The man goes into the next room. Immediately there is the sound of firing: Bang! Bang! Bang! This is followed by the sounds of a violent struggle, the smashing of glass and the scream of a woman. The man returns to the office and calmly places the gun on the desk. 'What happened?' asks the Head. The candidate replies, 'The gun you gave me was loaded with blanks, sir. So I threw her out of the window!'

A marriage where not only esteem, but passion is kept awake, is, I am convinced, the most perfect state of happiness: but it requires great care to keep this tender plant alive (Frances Brooke).

This is the letter which Liz sent to Brian last summer. 'Dear Brian, I have been unable to sleep since I broke off our engagement. Won't you forgive and forget? Your absence is breaking my heart. Nobody can take your place. I love you. All my love forever, Liz. PS Congratulations on becoming a Lotto millionaire!'

Partnership, not dependence, is the real romance of marriage (Murial Fox).

Last week I ran into Jim as he was coming out of the art gallery. We chatted over lunch when he dropped a bombshell on me. 'Steve,' he said, 'Alice and I are going to get a divorce.' I was stunned. 'Why? What happened? You two seemed so happy together.' 'Well,' he said, 'ever since we got married, my wife has tried to change me. She got me to stop drinking, smoking, swearing and so much more. She taught me to dress well, enjoy the fine arts, gourmet cooking, classical music and the ballet.' 'Are you bitter because she spent so much time trying to change you?' I probed. 'Oh not at all,' he replied, 'Now that I'm so improved and refined, she just isn't good enough for me.'

It usually takes some time for the husband and wife to know each other's humours and habits, and to find out what surrender of their own they can make with the least reluctance for their mutual good (Amelai Opie).

Billy comes home from school and proudly announces that he's been given a part in the school play. 'I play a man who has been married for twenty years,' he says. 'Don't worry,' replies his father, ' Keep up the good work and next time they may give you a speaking part.'

After a difficult few months a couple are visiting RELATE, when the wife confides to the marriage counsellor, 'The only reason we are still married is because neither of us want custody of the children.'

A man dies and his wife phones to place an announcement in the local newspaper. She asks to be put through to the Births, Marriages and Deaths department, and says, 'I want you to print: Fred is dead. The man at the newspaper says, 'But for the minimum charge of £8 you are allowed to print six words.' The woman replies, 'OK. Then print: Fred is dead. Jaguar for sale.'

An archaeologist is the best husband a woman can have. The older she gets, the more interested he is in her.

There are only two things that are absolute realities, love and knowledge, and you can't escape them
(Ella Wheeler Wilcox).

A rich man is approached by a beggar asking for food. The rich man says, 'Do you smoke? I could give you some of my finest Havana cigars.' The beggar replies, 'No, I don't. I am hungry and want food.' The rich man then asks, 'Do you drink? I have a bottle of vintage champagne which you could have.' The beggar replies, 'No, I don't. I am hungry and want food.' The rich man then asks, 'Do you gamble? I have contacts at Newmarket and I could give you some surefire tips for the races this weekend.' The beggar again replies, 'No, I don't. I am hungry and want food.' Finally, the rich man says, 'Well in that case I had better take you back to my mansion.' He invites the beggar into his Porsche and drives him to his very substantial home, where he introduces the beggar to his wife. She takes her husband to one side and asks, 'Why have you brought this poor man here? Are you going to invite him to live with us, to eat our food and to wear our clothes?' 'No, of course not,' the rich man replies, 'I just wanted to show you what happens to a man who doesn't smoke, drink or gamble.'

Marriage turns a night owl into a homing pigeon (Glenn Shelton).

Zoe could be quite devious at school. I remember the time I asked her what the 'F' meant on her school report, and she said, 'Fantastic.'

What do you instantly know about a well-dressed man? His wife is good at choosing clothes.

It is a truth universally acknowledged, that a single man in possession of good fortune, must be in want of a wife (Jane Austen, opening words of *Pride and Prejudice*).

Love understands love; it needs no talk (Frances Ridley Havergal).

An elderly couple return from a wedding and are in a pretty romantic mood. While sitting on the couch, the elderly woman looks at her husband and says, 'I remember when you used to hold my hand at every opportunity.' The old man, feeling obligated, reaches over and gently places his hand upon hers. Then she says, 'I also remember when you used to kiss me every time you had the opportunity.' The old man, again feeling obligated, leans over and gives her a peck on the cheek. The elderly woman then says, 'And I also remember when you used to nibble on my neck and send chills down my spine.' This time the old man stands up and begins to walk out of the room. His wife asks, 'Was it something I said? Where are you going?' The old man looks back at her and replies, 'I'm going in the bathroom to get my teeth.'

Marriage is when a man and woman become one. The trouble starts when they try to decide which one.

Love and hope are twins (Maria Brooks).

A recently married young couple are in their honeymoon suite. As they undress for bed, the burly husband tosses his trousers to his bride and says, 'Put these on.' She steps into them and finds they are twice the size of her body. 'I can't wear your trousers,' she says. 'That's right!' exclaims the husband, 'And don't you forget it. I'm the one who wears the trousers in this family!' At this, she removes her scanty panties and throws them to her husband. 'Try these on,' she says. He tried them on and finds he can only get them on as far as his knees. 'I can't get into your panties,' he says. 'That's right!' she exclaims, 'And you never will until your attitude changes.'

A newly married woman asks her husband, 'Do you want dinner?' 'What are the choices,' he asks. 'Yes or no,' she replies.

A rich man asks his wife, 'Darling, what would you like for your birthday present? How about a diamond ring?' 'I don't care much for diamonds,' she replies. 'Well, how about a mink coat?' he asks. 'You know I don't like furs,' she replies. 'A golden necklace?' he suggests. 'I already have five of them,' she replies. 'Well, darling, what *do* you want?' he enquires. 'What I'd really like is a divorce,' she answers. He thinks about things for a moment or two, and then says, 'Hmmm, I wasn't planning on spending *that* much.'

Marriage is our last, best chance to grow up (Joseph Barth).

When you are in love, you tell each other a thousand things without talking (Hawaiian proverb).

After thirty years of marriage, a woman becomes tired of being continually ignored by her husband. When he comes home from work, she says, 'Hello, darling. Notice anything different about me today?' 'Oh, I don't know,' he says, 'have you had your hair done?' 'No.' she says, 'Try again.' 'Well, maybe you've bought a new dress,' he says. 'No,' she says, 'Keep trying.' 'You've had your nails done,' he says. 'No, try again,' she continues. 'I give up, I'm too tired to play Twenty Questions!' he snarls. And she says, 'I'm wearing a gas mask!'

My wife is very dear to me ... she costs me a fortune.

A young man, looking to get married, confides in his friend, 'The problem is: my mother doesn't get on with any of the women I bring home. What can I do?' 'Oh, that's easy,' his friend replies, 'Find someone who's just like your mother.' 'I tried that last week,' the young man says, 'and my father hated her.'

Love is life, love is the lamp that lights the universe: without that light this goodly frame the earth, is a barren promontory and man the quintessence of dust (Mary Elizabeth Braddon).

Ryan, when you have a discussion with your new wife, always remember to get the last two words in: 'Yes, dear!'

At dinner, a newlywed wife says to her husband, 'The two things I cook best are chicken curry and apple pie.' To which the husband replies, 'Which is this?'

Married life can be very frustrating. In the first year of marriage, the man speaks and the woman listens. In the second year, the woman speaks and the man listens. In the third year, they both speak and the neighbours listen.

A husband comes home and finds his wife, dressed in a raincoat and an anorak, painting the living room. He asks her why she is wearing these clothes in the house and she replies, 'I read the can, and it said, " for best results put on two coats." '

Marriage is so popular because it combines the maximum of temptation with the maximum of opportunity (George Bernard Shaw).

The bride, upon her engagement, rushes to her mother, and says, 'I've found a man just like dad!' Her mother replies, 'So what do you want from me ... sympathy?'

A successful marriage is an edifice that must be rebuilt every day (André Maurois).

Love remoulds the world nearer to the heart's desire (Mary Berenson).

A married couple are going through a very difficult period so they decide to visit a marriage counsellor. After they have talked for a while, the counsellor says to the husband, 'You are very stressed and you need some space. I suggest that you run five miles every day next week, then call me back.' A week later the counsellor receives a call from the husband. 'Well,' she asks, 'how are you getting on with your wife?' 'How should I know?' says the husband, 'I'm thirty-five miles away.'

Whenever you're wrong, admit it; whenever you're right, shut up (Ogden Nash).

When a man opens the door of his car for his wife, you can be sure of one thing: either the car is new, or the wife.

If love does not know how to give and take without restrictions, it is not love, but a transaction that never fails to lay stress on a plus or a minus (Emma Goldman).

A young couple return from their honeymoon and finally put away all the presents they had received a fortnight earlier from their extended families and numerous friends. The next day, they receive two tickets in the post for a top West End show for which you couldn't normally get tickets for love nor money. Attached to the tickets is a small piece of paper with this single line: 'Guess Who Sent These?' The couple have much fun trying to identify the donor, but fail in the effort. They go to London and have a wonderful time. On their return home, in the early hours of the next morning, still trying to identify their unknown host, they find the house stripped of every item of value. On the bare table in the dining room is a piece of paper on which is written, in the same hand as on the note which accompanied the tickets: 'Now You Know!'

It doesn't matter how often a married man changes his job, he still ends up with the same boss.

Before we got married, my wife promised to sew, clean and cook ... and she did. She sowed her wild oats, cleaned me out, and cooked my goose.

A couple are celebrating their thirtieth wedding anniversary, when the wife bluntly asks, 'Did you marry me because you heard my great-uncle had left me a fortune?' And the husband replies, 'Of course not, dear. I'd have married you no matter who had left you the money.'

To celebrate their ruby wedding anniversary, a couple decide to spent a weekend in Wales. When they arrive at their hotel, the receptionist says, 'Sorry, we only have the honeymoon suite available.' 'My wife and I have been married for 40 years,' the man says, 'We don't need the honeymoon suite.' 'Don't panic, sir,' replies the receptionist, 'If I were to rent you the Millennium Stadium, you wouldn't have to play rugby!'

Marriage is like wine. It gets better with age (Dudley Moore).

I had been married for three years, but never told anyone. I like to keep my troubles to myself.

If you want your wife to listen and pay strict attention to every word you say, talk in your sleep.

In all the years I've been married, I've never stopped being romantic. If my wife ever finds out, I'm dead.

The heart can do anything (French proverb).

Just imagine, if it weren't for marriage, men would go through life thinking they had no faults at all.

The only true happiness in life is to love and be loved (George Sand).

A man leaves the snow-covered streets of London for a holiday in Australia. His wife is on a business trip and is planning to join him there that weekend. When he reaches his hotel, he decides to send his wife a quick email. Unable to find the scrap of paper on which he has written her email address, he does his best to type it in from memory. Unfortunately, he misses one letter and his message is directed to an elderly vicar's wife, whose husband has passed away only the day before. When the grieving widow checks her emails, she takes one look at the monitor, lets out a piercing scream and drops dead on the spot. Hearing the thud, her family rush into the room and see this message on the screen. It reads: 'Dearest wife, Had a good journey. Just got checked in. Everything prepared for your arrival here on Friday. PS It's really hot down here.'

A successful marriage involves falling in love many times - but always with the same person (Bob Monkhouse).

The newlywed bride says to her husband, 'I'm not cleaning up after you. I'm a career woman. That means I pay others to do the housework.' 'How much do you pay?' he asks. And she replies, '£6.50 an hour. Take it or leave it.'

Love is not getting, but giving. It is sacrifice. And sacrifice is glorious! (Marie Dressler).

I was crazy to get married ... but I didn't realise it at the time.

A man takes his wife along to a marriage counsellor. The counsellor asks him to explain their problem. The man says, 'What's 'er name here claims I don't pay her enough attention.'

Dawn love is silver,
Wait for the west:
Old love is gold love -
Old love is best (Katherine Lee Bates).

May your love for each other grow as surely as your waist-lines will.

Whoever loves true life, will love true love
(Elizabeth Barrett Browning).

There is no more lovely, friendly and charming relationship,
communion or company than a good marriage (Martin Luther).

Several men are sitting around the locker room after
their Saturday morning workout at the gym. Suddenly a
mobile phone on one of the benches rings and a man
picks it up. A woman says, 'Hi, darling it's me. Are you at
the gym?' 'Yes,' he replies. 'Great!' she continues, 'I've just
seen the ideal dress for the party. It costs £600, but
you'll love it. Can I buy it?' The man replies, 'Well if you like
it that much, of course you can.' 'Wonderful,' she says,
'And I've found the perfect cruise for next summer. It's
£6,000. But we'll travel everywhere we've ever talked
about. There's only two places left. What do you think?'
And the man says, 'Sure, book it right now.' 'Before you
hang up, darling,' the woman continues, 'that dream
house we looked at last year is back on the market again.
They're asking £600,000. I know it's a lot, but we'll never
get another chance like this!' 'Right,' says the man, 'we
don't want to lose it again. Offer the full price and say
we'll complete within a month!' 'Oh, darling, you're
wonderful! I love you! See you later,' she says. The man
hangs up, holds the mobile above his head and asks all
those present, 'Whose phone is this?'

Love is the wine of existence (Henry Ward Beecher).

A toast: May my wonderful daughter one day be blessed
with rich parents!

The great secret of a successful marriage is to treat all disasters as incidents and none of the incidents as disasters (Harold Nicolson).

A prisoner in jail receives a letter from his wife. It reads: 'Dear husband, I have decided to grow some cabbages in the back garden. When is the best time to plant them?' The prisoner, knowing the guards read all the mail, replies in a letter: 'Dear wife, whatever you do, do not touch the back garden. That is where I hid the money.' A week later, the prisoner receives another letter from his wife. It says: 'Dear husband, today some men came with spades to the house and dug up all the back garden.' The prisoner writes back: 'Dear wife, now is the best time to plant the cabbages.'

Men who have pierced ears are better prepared for married life ... because they have already bought cheap jewellery and experienced ears of pain.

In the arithmetic of love, one plus one equals everything and two minus one equals nothing (Mignon McLaughlin).

True love is like the misty rain that falls so softly, yet floods the river (Nigerian proverb).

Love is a great force in life; it is indeed the greatest of all things (E.M. Forster).

It is 3 o'clock in the morning and a husband and wife are asleep, when suddenly the phone rings. The husband picks up the phone and says, 'Hello? ... How the hell should I know? What am I, a weatherman?' And he slams the phone down. His wife rolls over and asks, 'Who was that?' Her husband replies, 'I don't know. Some guy who wanted to know if the coast was clear.'

When (daughter) was about four she came home from nursery one day and said, 'My teacher is silly.' 'What do you mean she's silly?' I asked. 'Well when I put my shoes on today, teacher said "(daughter), you've put your shoes on the wrong feet." That's why teacher is silly ... because I know they are my feet.'

On the first day of infant school, about mid-morning, the teacher turned to the class and said, 'If anyone has to go to the toilet, put your hand in the air.' (Daughter) stood up and asked, 'How will that help?'

When (daughter) first went to uni, (wife) was rather concerned about her and warned her over and over again never to take any boys back to her room. At the end of the Christmas term, when (daughter) came home, she told (wife) that she had met (groom). 'I hope you haven't taken him back to your room,' (wife) exclaimed. 'No, mum,' (daughter) replied. 'I know how much you'd have worried if I' done that ... I always go back to his room ... let his mum do the worrying.'

8 Sample Speeches

Finally, it's time to put it all together by taking a look at some full length speeches. While you may decide to adapt, personalise, and possibly combine what you consider to be the best bits, the main reason for including them in this final chapter is to remind you of the style and tone you should adopt throughout your speech. Your address should be emotional and sentimental, yet enlivened with touches of humour. It should also be *short*.

In the Bible, the story of the Creation is told in 400 words (that's less than 3 minutes) and the Ten Commandments are covered in less than 300. Try to say everything you need to in around 700 to 1,400 words. Each of the speeches that follow would take about five minutes to deliver.

Stand up to be seen ... Speak up to be heard ... Sit down to be appreciated!

Sample Speech 1

Reverend Jones, Ladies and Gentlemen - Friends, 'We cannot fully enjoy life unless someone we love enjoys it with us.' Not my words, I'm afraid, although how I agree with them.

This is a truly historic day! This day, the 13th of July, will always be remembered for three world famous events. Film actor Harrison Ford was born in 1942; Live Aid concerts raised millions for charity back in 1985; and on this day in 201X, Richard married Karen!

I cannot begin to tell you how delighted I am to see my daughter, Karen, looking so radiant as she begins a new chapter of her life - as wife and partner of Richard. I know I'm also speaking for Mary when I say we are not losing Karen; we are merely entrusting her to Richard's care.

And as we have got to know Richard well over the last few months, we have come to the inescapable conclusion that this will be very good care. He has shown himself to be exactly the sort of person we had always hoped Karen would marry. He is really likeable and easy going, hard working, and he has immaculate tastes. After all, he supports United and he chose Karen, didn't he? We are delighted to welcome him formally into our family, and I hope that he is now pleased to be a member of the Matthew clan. What we find gratifying is that Richard's parents feel the same about Karen. They have taken her to their hearts, and I believe that she is a real favourite with Jack and Babs.

Mary and I are really fortunate that the second of our lovely daughters has made a match with her Mr. Right, and indeed, as with her sister, in doing so, has brought more welcome people into our family. Of course, marriage is not only about finding the perfect partner, but also about being one. I believe that marriage will teach Richard, loyalty, self-restraint, and control. It will develop in him a sense of fair play … and many other qualities … which he wouldn't need if he had stayed single!

You know, it seems like only yesterday that I found Karen playing with her new teaset. 'Are you washing the dishes?' I asked. 'Yes,' she replied, 'and I'm drying them as well because I'm not married yet.' Richard, you have been warned! In those days, Karen's weekends were taken up with tap dancing, ballet and the pony club. She called her pony Radish and used to go round telling everyone it was her horse Radish.

As many of you know, Karen has always been a hard-working girl and she had a series of part-time jobs that helped her through college. Not long after she began working for Clareys the Cleaners, her office manager made a spot check of her work. 'Look at this desk!' he exclaimed, 'It looks as if it hasn't been cleaned in a month.' 'You can't blame me for that,' replied Karen, 'I've only worked here for a fortnight.'

Then there was the time she worked in a florists. She had to put all the little messages on the flowers, but got them mixed up. The flowers going to a wedding had a funeral card on them saying, 'With deepest sympathy.' And on the flowers for a funeral, she put a card, saying, 'Hope you'll be happy in your new home ...' Well, today it's my turn to wish you both the happiest of times together in *your* new home!

To be serious for a moment, I know that we suggested that you should elope and have your wedding on a beach in the Bahamas, but we're so glad you didn't, because this has been a wonderful wedding day, and it's not over yet!

It is customary on an occasion such as this for the father of the bride to offer the newlyweds some profound piece of advice, so here goes ... Happy marriages begin when we marry the one we love ... they blossom when we love the one we married. When children find true love, parents find true joy. Here's to your joy and ours from this day forward. Ladies and Gentlemen, please stand, raise your glasses and drink a toast with me to the health and happiness of Richard and Karen.

To Richard and Karen!

Sample Speech 2

Ladies and Gentlemen, Winston Churchill was apparently once asked to address a prep school and he got up and said, 'Never, Never, Never give up!' then sat down. Well you are not going to get away quite as easily as that, but I will try to be brief.

I'd like to start by welcoming, on behalf of Alice and Victoria, David and the guests of both of our families. Some of you have travelled a long way to be here today, but whether your journey was 12,000 miles or 2 miles we thank you all sincerely for being here to share this special day with us. I've met some of David's family for the first time, and I think we've all hit it off really well.

David knew I'd be nervous addressing so many people today, especially those of you I hadn't met before, so he told me this little story to remind me how quickly friendships can be forged. A girl he knew was waiting for a bus. She realised that when it came she would have trouble climbing aboard in her very tight skirt. So she reached surreptitiously behind her and loosened the zip. When the bus arrived, the man behind her in the queue, picked her up by the waist and placed her on it. 'How dare you!' she exclaimed. And he said, 'Well, after you opened my flies, I thought we were friends.' From the way we're all getting on so well today, I think we are friends too!

I'd now like to take the opportunity to thank the beautiful bridesmaids for looking after Victoria, the Vicar for a lovely service, her Boss for the great weather, and the staff of Kandinskis for the excellent food and service.

Weddings don't just happen. They take a fantastic amount of hard work , organisation ... and money! Of course, this is my daughter's big day and, quite rightly, no one here is paying much attention to me. But I can assure you that I'm getting my fair share of attention elsewhere. My bank manager, my mortgage lender, and several credit card companies are watching me extremely carefully. Today, we haven't lost a daughter ... we've gained an overdraft. Only joking ... I think ... but I would like to ask you all to join me in a toast to Alice, as without her constant hard work over several months, today would not have gone nearly as well as it has. My wife – Alice. Any excuse for a drink!

It was 1982 when Vikki made her entrance into this world. She immediately brightened up our lives and has continued to do so ever since. You never did learn to turn off the lights did you? Dave is also very important to us and in the seven years that we have known him, Alice and I have seen the strength of his character, his warmth and his great ability to make Victoria happy.

I know we live in a sometimes crazy, mixed-up world, but days like this somehow seem to make sense of it all to me. In the words of that famous song from Vikki's favourite film, *Casablanca*:

'It's still the same old story,
A fight for love and glory,
A case of do or die!
The world will always welcome lovers.
As time goes by.'

Today the world welcomes David and Victoria!

Well, finally I would like to return to Winston Churchill and my serious advice to you both: 'Never, Never, Never give up' ... on loving each other and on working together to make your marriage last and become everything that you both want and deserve.

It now gives me great pleasure to propose a toast to the long life together and the happiness of Victoria and David.

Ladies and Gentlemen, The bride and groom!

Sample Speech 3

Ladies and Gentlemen, as father of the bride, it is my privilege to make the first speech and I would like to start by saying what a real pleasure it is to welcome, on this joyous occasion, Liz and Joe, John's parents, together with relatives and friends of both families.

Today, we, on the top table, are surrounded by most of the friends and family who have been so important to us during our lives. Some have travelled hundreds of miles, just to be here today. On behalf of John and Paula, Liz and Joe, and Ethel and I – we welcome you all and thank you sincerely for your friendship and support over many years – and for sharing this special day with us. By your presence, you show friendship and love, and bring even greater joy to us all.

We are very proud today to see Paula – looking so beautiful – now married to John. During the time we have known him, we have come to realise how special John is to Paula, and anyone can see that they are made for each other. He is really likeable and easy going, and we are very happy to welcome him formally into the family, and as a member of the Owen clan.

John, as someone with some experience of marriage, I would like to warn you about what you'll be up against. I didn't think it wise to say anything before you'd gone through with the wedding, in case you chickened out! There's something you'll have to learn to live with, because no man has yet found a remedy for it; and that is, the female mind.

I remember the time when Ethel bought me two ties for my birthday, a red one and a blue one. I was undecided as to which one to wear at the party that evening, but appeared in the red one. As soon as Ethel saw me, she said, 'Oh! you're wearing the red tie. Don't you like the blue one?' John, sometimes you just can't win!

And what about my delightful daughter? Doesn't she look magnificent? You know, it seems like only yesterday when I stormed into Paula's bedroom and told her to turn off that dreadful heavy metal CD. 'Why, do you want to borrow it?' she asked ... Come to think of it, it was yesterday! But seriously, Paula is the best daughter a man could ever wish for ... she is intelligent, beautiful, thoughtful ... in fact she does everything for me. She even wrote this speech!

Isn't it funny how the meaning of words change over time? For example, we all know how the meaning of the word gay has changed over the years. The older generation is not always aware of such changes, as this little story will illustrate. When John and Paula got engaged, I said to John, 'I expect you'll be saving your pennies from now on. You don't need to spend a fortune to enjoy yourself. Why don't you do what Ethel and I did when we were first engaged and money was tight? Ethel and I used to be perfectly happy going out for a walk in the park on a pleasant summer evening. We used to call that 'going for a bit of a blow', which I now, understand from John's sniggers, may have a slightly different meaning to young people today!

It is customary on an occasion such as this for the father of the bride to pass on some words of wisdom about the institution of marriage. Well, if 35 years of blissful marriage has taught me anything, it is this: If you would have a happy family life, remember two things – in matters of principle, stand like a rock – in matters of taste, swim with the current.

Handing Paula to John, reminds me of what has been said of relationships:

If you love something, set it free.

If it comes back, it was, and always will be, yours.

If it never returns, it was never yours to begin with.

And, if all it does is... just sit in your house, mess up your stuff, spend your money, eat your food, use the telephone all night, and monopolise your television.... you either married it, or gave birth to it!

Ladies and Gentlemen, there are only two lasting bequests parents can hope to give their children ... one of these is roots and the other is wings. Paula, I believe that over the years we have given you strong roots. Today, Ethel and I know the time is right for you to fly away from the nest with John. Ladies and Gentlemen – Friends, it is now my pleasant duty to propose a toast to the happy couple…. to the love birds … to John and Paula!

To John and Paula!

A Final Word

… and so we face the final curtain. The bottom line is be yourself and allow your natural personality to shine through. As Sinatra put it: say the things you truly feel, and not the words of one who kneels. Say them proudly … say them emotionally … say them humorously. But more, much more than this, say them *your* way!

Printed in Great Britain
by Amazon